BEDFORD BUSES AND COACHES

HOWARD BERRY

AMBERLEY

First published 2021

Amberley Publishing
The Hill, Stroud
Gloucestershire, GL5 4EP

www.amberley-books.com

Copyright © Howard Berry, 2021

The right of Howard Berry to be identified as
the Author of this work has been asserted in
accordance with the Copyrights, Designs and
Patents Act 1988.

ISBN 978 1 4456 7568 8 (print)
ISBN 978 1 4456 7569 5 (ebook)

British Library Cataloguing in Publication Data.
A catalogue record for this book is available from
the British Library.

Typesetting by Aura Technology and Software
Services, India. Printed in the UK.

Contents

Introduction

Bedford's origins go back to 1857 when Alexander Wilson founded a pump and marine engine manufacturing business in the South London district of Vauxhall. In 1863, a Mr Betts Brown purchased the company and began manufacturing travelling cranes, renaming the company Vauxhall Iron Works. In 1903, the manufacture of motor cars commenced and shortly afterwards the company relocated to Luton in Bedfordshire, the county the company was to call its home. The move into manufacturing commercial and passenger vehicles came about when the American company General Motors purchased Vauxhall in 1925. Prior to this date, General Motors had been assembling lorries in Britain from parts manufactured in its Canadian plant under Imperial Preference, a system of free trade agreements between the various colonies of what was the British Empire. The vehicles were assembled at a factory in Hendon, North London, under the name British Chevrolet. With the purchase of Vauxhall, production was transferred from Hendon to Luton, and taking the name of the county town of Bedfordshire, Bedford Motors was established.

By the start of Second World War, Bedford had become a major supplier to the British Army. In preparation for the main assault for D-Day, Vauxhall were asked by the Ministry of Production to produce the Churchill tank. This required the company to build additional production space but needed government funding to do so. This was agreed, and a new 98-acre site in Dunstable was built in 1942, which featured a rail connection to bring the raw materials in and take the finished products out. In the 1950s, all large commercial and passenger vehicle production was moved from Luton to Dunstable, and between 1955 and 1957 General Motors invested in two new 800,000-square-foot, double-storey factories covering 46 acres, with a production line 1 mile long and employing over 5,500 people. Military vehicles remained Bedford's biggest market with huge contracts for the British forces. However, by the 1980s the factory was downsizing and shedding jobs as it was dealt a big blow when the company failed to win a major contract to supply the MOD with its standard 4-ton 4x4 GS (general service) truck for the British forces. This was despite the Bedford candidate performing equally as well as the British Leyland vehicle, and the British Army expressing a preference to continue with their trusted relationship with Bedford. There are many theories behind the decision, most of them political, as the contract was seen by the government of the day as being essential for the long-term survival of Leyland.

The failure to gain such a huge contract, combined with the general decline in the sales of civilian lorries, buses and coaches, led to General Motors making the announcement in September 1986 that heavy commercial and passenger vehicle production was to end, and the Dunstable site was to be sold. In 1987, both the site and business were sold to entrepreneur David J. B. Brown, with vehicles to be badged as AWD (General Motors was retaining the Bedford name for light vans, which continued to be produced at Luton). AWD continued to build the TL and TM range of lorries, as well as a version of the TK lorry for the military. However, cheaper competition from abroad saw AWD enter receivership in 1992, and the brand was bought by Marshall of Cambridge, with the Dunstable site being redeveloped by the receiver; a sad end to a company whose products were so popular they even said 'you see them everywhere'.

As an aside, Vauxhall and Bedford's logo was a griffin, which was derived from the heraldic crest of Falkes de Breauté, who was granted the Manor of Luton by King John. By marriage, he acquired property in London, known as Fulk's Hall, which over time came to be known as Vauxhall, the original home of the company.

Whilst my association with Bedford coaches only lasted for a few years, I came to respect the marque immensely, both for its versatility and reliability. Indeed, I only suffered one breakdown in a Bedford and that was due to the failure of a proprietary product, and not with the vehicle itself. I was recently lucky enough to be taken to an event on the superb Plaxton Paramount-bodied YNT, still owned and operated by Roy McCarthy Coaches of Macclesfield, and as soon as the door closed and the clutch was dipped, all those familiar Bedford noises came flooding back.

With such a wide range of vehicles to write about, and only a limited amount of space to do it in, I decided to only include those models I had first-hand experience of, and so contained within are chapters on the VAL, VAM and Y Series. The story is told through 180 colour photographs with what are (hopefully) informative and sometimes humorous captions. As with my previous publications I have been greatly assisted in my endeavours by a handful of photographers to whom I am indebted, not only for letting me use their work, but also for having the foresight to record these vehicles in their heyday for others to enjoy so many years later. Each photographer has an initialled credit after their work, and are Alan Snatt (AS), Martyn Hearson (MH), Richard Simons (RS), Terry Walker (TW) and Paul Green (PG). Finally, talking of initials, within the photo captions NBC refers to the National Bus Company, and SBG to the Scottish Bus Group.

Howard Berry
Cheswardine
Shropshire

The VAL

In July 1961, the maximum PSV chassis dimensions in the UK were increased from 30 ft length to 36 ft and from 8 ft width to 8 ft 2.5 ins. width. The SB was already more or less stretched to its limits, so a fresh new design was called for, and that design – the Bedford VAL – was arguably the most recognised PSV chassis ever made. The VAL was introduced in 1962 and featured a twin steer arrangement which became known as the 'Chinese Six'. The VAL was the first Bedford chassis with an overhang ahead of the front wheels, allowing the passenger door to be fitted at the front of the vehicle. The original VAL, designated VAL14, was fitted with a front-mounted 6.17-litre Leyland O.400 engine and five-speed gearbox. Air pressure servo-assisted brakes operated on all six wheels with the added safety feature of an auxiliary brake mounted onto the propshaft, designed to stop the vehicle using the transmission rather than the brakes. In 1967, the VAL14 was replaced by the VAL70, with Bedford's own 7.6-litre 466 engine replacing the Leyland unit, and this was to remain the standard engine fitment until the end of production in 1973. There was reasoning behind the twin steer arrangement – the VAL was fitted with small 16-inch-diameter wheels, which not only led to reduced weight in wheels, suspension and steering equipment, but also brought along improved ride quality. Bedford was also able to use existing parts from the TK truck range, and so did away with the need to develop a new front axle.

The VAL featured in two iconic films of the era, with Harrington Legionnaire-bodied ALR 453B being used to transport the three Minis in *The Italian Job*, and Plaxton Panorama-bodied URO 913E featuring in the 1967 Beatles film *Magical Mystery Tour*. This coach was new to Fox of Hayes in 1967 and in the film was raced around RAF West Malling, driven by Ringo Starr. Such was the popularity of the VAL that a number are in preservation, indeed in some cases semi-preservation as one or two are still registered as PSVs and able to do a day's work if required. VAL production ended in 1973, by which time over 2,000 had been built, the majority for the home market but with some vehicles exported to Australia, New Zealand and Denmark.

Between 1948 and 1964, Loughborough-based coach dealer W. S. Yeates built some rather stylish bodies on a variety of chassis. The Yeates Europa was fitted to eleven VAL14s in 1963, seven of which were delivered to Barton of Chilwell. They were to a unique dual-door design as seen on 964 (964 RVO) on layover in Chilwell depot. (AS)

To people of a certain age, the Duple Vega Major-bodied VAL will rekindle memories of the Dinky Supertoys model, complete with battery-operated lights. Here, however, is the real thing, DME 976A, new in 1963 to Martin of Hillingdon, but now operating for BEA. (AS)

Whilst the Vega Major was immortalised in model form, probably the most famous VAL of all was the Harrington Legionnaire-bodied example filled with Mini Coopers for the film *The Italian Job*. Rather less exciting but still looking equally smart is Barton's Legionnaire-bodied VAL14 993 (993 VRR), one of eight delivered in 1964; the largest single delivery of Legionnaires out of the forty-two bodied on the VAL. (AS)

Formed in 1922, Seaview Services operated a successful bus service between Seaview and Ryde, with most passengers travelling to the holiday camps at Puckpool and St Clare. At the time it was the only stage carriage service on the Isle of Wight not operated by Southern Vectis. New in 1964, Duple (Midland)-bodied VAL14 ADL 321B is seen on Ryde Esplanade in 1970. (AS)

North Western's Altrincham to Warrington service was a pleasant countryside ride; however the low bridge under the Bridgewater Canal at Dunham Massey posed quite an obstacle. To replace the previous low-height single deckers, ten Strachan-bodied VAL14s, with unusual curved rooflines, were delivered in 1964 and lasted for eight years until they were replaced by similarly rooved ECW-bodied Bristol REs in 1971. Seen in Northwich garage after withdrawal are 130/131/139 (AJA 130B etc.). (AS)

Isle of Man operator Corkill's Garage of Onchan were avid Bedford users and, if my information is correct, between 1950 and 1972, when Corkill's morphed into Tours (Isle of Man), they only operated one non-Bedford. Seen parked in Ramsay on excursion duties is Plaxton-bodied VAL14 8 (BMN 111), new in 1964 as 52 XNN to Thomas of North Muskham. (AS)

If you cut me in half, you'd find 'Yelloway' written through me like a stick of Blackpool rock, and whilst that legendary Rochdale-based company standardised on the AEC Reliance, between 1962 and 1969 they ordered one or two Bedfords every year, predominantly for use on the Clacton service. In 1965, four Legionnaire-bodied VAL14s arrived, two for the Creams subsidiary, and as seen here in Derby bus station, CDK 409/10C for the main Yelloway fleet. (AS)

Only six MCW Topaz II bodies were built on the VAL including FWW 809C, new to Billie's of Mexborough in 1965. By 1973, when it was caught leaving Doncaster South bus station whilst in the ownership of Millward of Sheffield, it seems to have had some major work to its roofline, resulting in the loss of two of the offside roof lights. (RS)

Another Topaz II having had its bodywork tampered with is JNK 686C. New to Fox of Hayes in 1965, it received a Duple Viceroy front panel and a set of bus seats whilst in the ownership of Jones of Login. (RS)

Seen outside the depot at Morton, Gainsborough is Eagre's Plaxton Panorama-bodied VAL14 GFU 444D, new in 1966 to Hudson of Horncastle. Useless fact time – Eagre was named after the Trent Aegir, which is a tidal bore on the River Trent that occurs when a high spring tide meets the downstream flow of the river and travels as far as Gainsborough. (RS)

Whilst better known for operating a large network of local bus services around the Winchester area, King Alfred Motor Services also had a small coach fleet, including Plaxton Panorama-bodied VAL14 EOU 703D, seen on an excursion to Eastbourne in 1969. (AS)

I wondered why Moss of Sandown's Duple Vega Major-bodied VAL14 EDL 783D carried a completely different livery to the rest of the fleet. After much research, I also cleared up the rather ambitious destination and why it carried the name *The New Yorker*. New in 1964, it was shipped to New York to be part of the General Motors display at that year's World Fair. It was not registered until after its return to the UK in 1966 and is seen here in 1970 on Ryde Esplanade. (AS)

Unaware of the international superstar it is passing is Southern Vectis 407 (HDL 230E), a 1967 Bedford VAL14 with Duple Viceroy 36 body. The Viceroy range was the replacement for the Bella range, of which the Vega Major (fitted onto EDL 783D) was the largest model. The front-end styling differences can be clearly seen. (AS)

For eighty-two years, between 1922 until 2004, Leon of Finningley operated not only stage carriage routes around the Doncaster area, but also ran a sizeable coaching fleet, the majority of new purchases being Bedfords. Two examples are seen here, Plaxton Panorama-bodied VAL14 LAL 547E leading Duple Bella Vega-bodied SB5 474 RRR past Doncaster South bus station. (RS)

Meanwhile, inside the bus station we find one of Leon's bus fleet. Willowbrook-bodied VAL14 OWW 686E was new in 1967 to near neighbour Wigmore of Dinnington and was acquired by Leon's in December 1970. It is seen in one of the parking bays going to the Nottinghamshire village of Misson, which interestingly is not directly accessible from the due to the route the River Idle takes through the village as the River Idle runs through it. (RS)

Certain Duple bodies had a reputation for being (how shall we say?) rather fragile, but this somewhat utilitarian Duple (Midland) bus body was certainly well travelled. JNT 252E was delivered to Dearneways of Goldthorpe but was never licensed, passing to Whittle of Highley (hence the Shropshire registration mark). Less than a year later it moved south to Wakes of Sparkford in Somerset, then passing to Brutonian in whose yard it is pictured. Full circle saw it return to South Yorkshire to join the fleet of Thistle Coaches, Doncaster. (RS)

Another superstar VAL was Fox of Hayes URO 913E, a 1967 Bedford VAL14 with Plaxton Panorama body. When seen in 1968, it was parked in Eastbourne's Susans Road coach station, surrounded by coaches from the Valliant Cronshaw fleet to whom it was running on hire. It was later immortalised on celluloid when a certain Mr Ringo Starr drove it round a racetrack in the Beatles 'film *Magical Mystery Tour*'. (AS)

I've included this picture of Duple Viceroy-bodied VAL70 MHU 926F, from the Wessex of Bristol fleet, because behind the coach is the bus stop where I used to catch the number 25 bus home from school and in later life I would go on to work for Wessex – albeit long after it ceased to be an independent coach operator. The location is just past the arches on Cheltenham Road in Bristol; the date is 1973. (RS)

Following the creation of the NBC, Wessex became part of National Travel (South West). Here we see MHU 926F again, this time during the transition period when vehicles were being painted from Wessex's red and grey livery into NBC white, as can be seen by the vehicles surrounding MHU. (RS)

I do love a classic street scene; it makes you realise just how much things have changed over the years. Not only has the National Westminster Bank morphed into the NatWest, but Woolworths is now just a high street memory. As well as two Minis and a Lancia, there are two sporty Ford Escorts; one a genuine RS2000 and the other fitted with some rather dubious wide wheel arches. Even if the vehicles including Duple Viceroy-bodied VAL70 SNV 777G of Holt of Newport were available, it would be impossible to recreate this scene as Boothferry Road in Goole is now pedestrianised. (RS)

Despite the name, Wilts & Dorset's operating territory was mainly Southern Wiltshire and Northern Hampshire, and in 1964 the company was merged with Bournemouth-based Hants & Dorset. Both companies became part of the NBC in 1969, and in 1972 it was announced that Hants & Dorset would be the name for the entire fleet. Despite being photographed after the announcement, the Wilts & Dorset fleet name and livery is very much in evidence in Basingstoke, where Duple Viceroy-bodied VAL70s 57 and 61 (PEL 905G and SEL 756H) wait their next turn of duty. (AS)

Introduced into the UK market in 1969, Portuguese-built Caetano bodywork (marketed through Moseley of Loughborough) rapidly established itself in the British coaching scene. Grayline of Bicester entered Caetano Estoril-bodied VAL70 TBW 718G into the 1969 Brighton Coach Rally. It is seen during the driving tests on Madeira Drive only days after delivery in April 1969. I imagine the passengers just loved sitting on those vinyl-covered seats on a scorching hot summer's day. (AS)

Caetano Estoril-bodied VAL70 VAA 107H was new to Cowdrey of Gosport in 1970. It is seen here providing a bit of luxury to the passengers using Daisy of Broughton's stage carriage service from Scunthorpe and is loading at the rear of the Lincolnshire Road Car depot in the town. (RS)

WR&P Bingley of Kinsley were one of the three members of the United Services consortium who operated local bus services around the Wakefield and Doncaster areas, all of which were conductor operated, even after the fleet was taken over by West Yorkshire PTE. They also had a sizeable coaching fleet including Plaxton Panorama Elite-bodied VAL70 DWW 431H, seen parked at Doncaster racecourse. (RS)

Another company taken over by West Yorkshire PTE was Baddeley Brothers of Holmfirth, whose approach to solving staff retention problems was to purchase houses which were rented to the staff at a nominal rent. Whenever a new vehicle was purchased, a book was started for it in which every item of its life was recorded, and when the vehicle was sold the book was passed on to the new owner. VAL 70 109 (JWT 725J) was a very early recipient of the mark II version of Plaxton's Panorama Elite body. (RS)

A company very much still with us is Thornes of Bubwith, whose immaculate fleet of preserved coaches are a familiar sight on today's rally scene. One vehicle which is long gone from the fleet though is Plaxton Panorama Elite-bodied VAL70 RAR 679J. It is included here to show the detail differences between the original Panorama Elite and the Mk II in the previous picture. (RS)

NJY 992J, a 1971 VAL70 with Duple Viceroy body, was acquired by Wallace Arnold with the business of Embankment of Plymouth. When Wallace Arnold's livery changed from cream to grey and white in 1970, Devon-based vehicles retained the cream, in part due to their main competitor in the day excursion market being Grey Cars of Torquay. It is seen on tour duties at Eastbourne's Princes Park coach park in 1975. (AS)

To finish off the VAL chapter we see the depot of Wilson of Whitburn, who traded as Economic. All parked up safely under cover are three Roe-bodied AEC Reliances in the background, with two Duple Vega Major-bodied Bedford VAL14s nearest the camera. Closest is 535 MUP, new in 1964, with FUP 440C from 1965 alongside. (RS)

The VAM

I mentioned in the previous chapter that the VAL was the first Bedford PSV chassis to have the door ahead of the front axle, although this is not strictly true as, to be pedantic, it was the first official Bedford chassis to have such a configuration. In the early 1960s, Loughborough-based bodybuilders Yeates converted some SB chassis to forward entrance by moving the axle backwards. Bedford didn't sanction this as an approved conversion for fears the body structure would be compromised due to the lack of front chassis rails to support the engine, door and driver. However, it became apparent that operators wanted a mid-sized front entrance vehicle, ideally for use in areas where the longer VAL would struggle to serve. In August 1965, Bedford commenced production of such a chassis, designated as the VAM. Unlike the VAL, with its two designations, the 10-metre-long VAM originally had three, depending on the engine fitted: VAM3 with a Bedford 300 petrol engine, VAM5 with a Bedford 330 diesel engine and the VAM14 fitted with a Leyland O.400 diesel engine. However, in 1967 the VAM14 was replaced by the VAM70, now fitted with the larger Bedford 466 diesel engine, but like the VAL, they were all mounted at the front of the vehicle and intruded into the saloon. The VAM3 was offered with either a Turner four- or five-speed gearbox, whilst the diesel-engined chassis had a five-speed box as standard.

Whilst the VAL was designed to carry up to fifty-five passengers, the shorter VAM was intended for bodywork able to carry up to forty-five passengers, and as such was an ideal vehicle for stage carriage use, but was equally at home when fitted with a coach body for touring and private hires. It sold extensively in the United Kingdom as well as abroad, with Cypriot operators being particularly enamoured with it, the VAM being available to this market long after it was replaced in the UK by the YRQ in 1970.

Whilst Wessex of Bristol was an independent operator, the fleet was 100 per cent Bedford, heavyweight coaches not joining the fleet until it became part of the NBC. The first front entrance Bedfords to join the fleet were a batch of five VAM5s fitted with Duple (Northern) Viscount bodies, delivered in 1965 but not entering service until 1966. EAE 933C is seen in Princes Park coach park, Eastbourne, in 1971. Apart from one of the batch that was written off in an accident, the rest lasted until 1976. (AS)

Grey Green were part of the George Ewer Group and operated a network of express services across East Anglia and the south coast resorts. 1966 Duple Bella Venture-bodied VAM14 JUV 528D discharges a healthy load at Eastbourne Junction Road coach station in 1972, the photographer seeming to have caught the attention of a couple of lovely ladies. (AS)

Eagle-eyed readers will notice that City of Oxford's Willowbrook-bodied VAM5 617 (FAW 157D) sports a Shropshire registration as well as a non-standard NBC destination display, with no facility for a route number. The bus was new to G. Cooper of Oakengates, near Telford, in 1966 and passed together with the rest of Cooper's fleet to Midland Red when Cooper was taken over in 1973. In 1975, its sister vehicle FAW 156D and two similarly bodied Bedford YRQs were transferred to Oxford, where it lasted less than a year before being sold for scrap. (RS)

Sheffield bus station in 1976 was probably as colourful (operator-wise) as it is today, with vehicles from Sheffield Corporation, Yorkshire Traction and two independents visible. Waiting to depart on the Sheffield United Tours service to Ingoldmells is Dearneways of Goldthorpe's Duple Viceroy-bodied VAM14 NDT 626E. The coach was new, in 1967, to Fretwells of Bentley – a fleet taken over by Dearneways in 1974 and who had a penchant for DT registration numbers – ten of the thirteen coaches delivered new all sporting the mark. (RS)

The dark green and black livery instantly identifies these 1967 Plaxton Panorama-bodied VAM14s as members of the Robinson's of Great Harwood fleet, whose vehicles were a familiar sight at coastal resorts when undertaking the company's extended tours. The Eastbourne tour must have been particularly popular to warrant two vehicles. Sister ships 139 & 140 (ATJ 139/140E) are seen here in the town's Princes Park coach station in 1971. (AS)

Despite its front engine intruding into the saloon, the VAM was popular as a service bus. However, only twenty-seven were bodied by Alexander, all 'Y Types', and all went to Scottish fleets. Eastern Scottish VAM14 C245K (HSF 245E) was delivered in 1967 and is seen turning from Edinburgh's St Andrew's Square bus station in 1971. (AS)

Nestled between a lovely pair of Bristols, Strachans Pacesaver II-bodied VAM5 KBC 214E of Ashdown Coaches of Burton is seen in Bridgwater bus station, having just arrived on the service from Stogursey and Cannington. It retains the livery, destination blind, fleet name and number of its previous owner, County Travel of Leicester, to whom it had been new in 1967. (RS)

You couldn't get a more 1970s Somerset scene if you tried: vehicles from Safeway Services, Hutchings & Cornelius and Southern National parked up, and Wakes of Sparkford's 1967 Duple Viceroy-bodied VAM14 MAX 225E pulling off the stand at Yeovil. Despite the lack of any destination display, it is clearly operating a local bus service as the driver wears crossed straps supporting cash bag and ticket machine. It was new to Sergeant of Rogerstone in South Wales and was acquired by Wakes in 1971. (RS)

Before MCW and Scania produced a double-deck bus of the same name, MCW produced thirty-three all-metal lightweight Metropolitan coach bodies between 1967 and 1970. PTG 242F was new to Edwards of Beddau in 1967 but is seen here in the ownership of York Motors of Manchester.

As seems to be the norm for the more rural subsidiaries of larger groups, Highland Omnibuses was the recipient of far more cascaded vehicles than new deliveries, including Duple Viceroy-bodied VAM5 HGM 32E, which was new to Central SMT in 1967. Resplendent in Highlands's grey and blue coaching livery, it is seen parked in Seafield Road depot, Inverness. (AS)

As well as coaches, Wilts & Dorset also had a small number of Bedfords for use on service work including this unusual dual-door Strachan-bodied VAM14. HHR 943E was delivered in 1967 as fleet number 813 but passed to Eagre, where it is seen parked in Gainsborough bus station. (RS)

Another Strachan's body and another street scene, this time outside Doncaster Racecourse in 1976, with a rather garishly painted PBD 931F – a VAM5 new to Arnold of Tamworth in 1966. The range of cars is very interesting, with most of the visible cars being of Continental manufacture, including a Lancia Beta, but what about the rather battered Armstrong Siddeley Sapphire on the left. (RS)

The BOAC terminal in the background harks back to the days when London's airports had no direct rail or tube links, with the main airlines, BEA and BOAC, providing inner London check-in points with coach transfers out to the airports. Across the road from the terminal is Victoria coach station, where Eastern Counties CB842 (PPW 842F), a 1968 Bedford VAM70 with Duple Viceroy bodywork, is seen arriving in 1968. (AS)

In 1967, the Tilling Group took delivery of twenty ECW-bodied VAMs for delivery to Western National, Eastern Counties and West Yorkshire Road Car, due to no alternative Bristol product following the end of MW and SU production. The rather sad-looking front-end design ensured the engine hump was not visible through the windscreen, whilst giving the driver some degree of kerbside visibility. Western National's VAM5 708 (KDV 138F) is seen in Newquay in 1972. (AS)

One of the most respected family owned coach operators in Britain was Epsom Coaches. Formed in 1920, and remaining in the Richmond family ownership until 2012, their maroon and cream coaches were a familiar sight across London. New in 1968 was OJU 636F, a VAM70 with Duple Viceroy body, seen loading for a tour to Holland at Tower Hill in London in 1969. (AS)

Formed in 1922 to operate bus services around Wakefield and Castleford, by the mid-1950s West Riding was the largest UK bus company in private hands. They also operated a sizeable coaching fleet. 27 (MHL 227F), a 1968 VAM70 with Plaxton Panorama body, pulls out of Belle Isle garage at Wakefield in 1968. Seen behind the VAM is a Guy Wulfrunian, West Riding being well known for their involvement in the ill-fated Wulfrunian project, operating 132 out of the 137 vehicles built. (AS)

Bournemouth-based Shamrock & Rambler was formed in 1924 as result of a merger between Shamrock Buses of Holton Heath near Poole and Bournemouth Rambler. It became company practice to give coaches names rather than fleet numbers, and when S&R became part of National Travel (South West) this continued, even though NBC policy dictated fleet numbers. 1968 Plaxton Panorama-bodied VAM70 423 (MHL 226F) carries the name *Wylye*, after the Wiltshire river. The coach was new to West Riding (sister vehicle to the previous picture) and is seen at the Aquarium Roundabout in Brighton in 1975. (AS)

The Eastern Scottish depot at Berwick-upon-Tweed was one of only two SBG depots in England, the Western Scottish depot at Carlisle being the other. Willowbrook dual-purpose-bodied VAM70 ZC269D (LFS 269F) is seen in Berwick in 1976 waiting to depart back to its home depot of Galashiels. (AS)

Seen at the opposite end of Scotland is Alexander (Northern) Duple-bodied VAM70 NW272 (JRS 472F). Northern Scottish, like other SBG companies, employed a system of codes to determine vehicle type, chassis make and depot allocation, the small MF plate to the left of the number plate indicating the coach was allocated to Macduff depot. (AS)

Formed in London in 1899, Birch Brothers originally operated horse buses before moving on to motor buses. In 1928, a service from London to Bedford commenced, and proved such a success that a depot was built in Rushden to operate services across the northern home counties. In 1959, the company was the first to operate a regular service from London on the newly opened M1 motorway, but a decline in passenger numbers saw the bus business sold to United Counties in 1969 and the coach operations to the Ewer Group two years later. Seen in Eastbourne's Susans Road coach station, when brand new in August 1969, is VAM70 VLF 38G fitted with a very early Plaxton Panorama Elite body. (AS)

In the early 1920s, HH Yeomans of Canon Pyon started using his cider lorry to carry passengers into Hereford for the Wednesday market, and by 1931 nineteen stage carriage services were being operated across Herefordshire. Today, the company operates a fleet of high-end touring coaches, as well as being the contract operator to National Express for the service between Hereford and London. Delivered in 1968 was 5 (PCJ 300G), a Willowbrook-bodied VAM70, seen at Canon Pyon depot in 1970. (AS)

At first glance looking like a Duple Viceroy, the stepped waistrail identifies this as another of the thirty-three MCW Metropolitan-bodied Bedfords. ROT 357G was new to Margo of Bexleyheath in May 1969 but is seen here at Linthwaite in April 1976 with local operator Kenmargra Coaches. One problem with low production bodies (as seen with the MCW Topaz earlier) is that when panels needed replacing, like for like replacements weren't available, hence the need to use alternatives. (TW)

As well as incumbent operator Midland Red, Gibson of Barlestone was one of several independents operating stage services into Leicester. Gibson's was formed in 1919 by brothers Walter and Edward Gibson – two miners who bought a bus to ferry themselves and their workmates to the local coalfields, parking the bus up whilst they did their shift before taking their colleagues home again. Between 1956 and 1979, when the company was sold to Leicester City Transport, only Bedfords were bought new with forty-two vehicles joining the fleet. Seen at The Newarke in April 1969 when brand new is 69 (PUT 617G), a Willowbrook-bodied VAM70. (AS)

You can tell it's a typical British seaside scene as everyone is wearing a coat. The Continental interloper, seen here at Brighton, is Caetano Cascais-bodied VAM70 EWR 551H of Camping's of Brighton. As mentioned earlier, Salvador Caetano of Portugal were amongst the first Continental bodybuilders to make serious inroads into the UK market through the deal with Loughborough-based dealers Moseley. The bodies were branded as Moseley Continentals, with Moseley using different model names depending on which chassis they were fitted to. (RS)

In 1972 the NBC introduced a corporate livery, which (with one or two notable exceptions) was poppy red or leaf green for buses and white for coaches. Vehicles capable of fulfilling dual roles had their bottom half in fleet colours and the top half painted white. This can be seen to good effect on Mansfield District's Duple Viceroy-bodied VAM70 28 (ERB 345H), seen at Marble Arch in London in 1973. (AS)

Laying over in Newcastle, deep in Northern General's operating territory and surrounded by buses from the Northern fleet, is Plaxton Derwent-bodied VAM70 VRM 100H from the fleet of Wright Bros of Nenthead. Although waiting to depart to Alston, the complete route the bus would later be operating was one of the longest single stage carriage services in Britain, a journey of 82 miles between Newcastle and Keswick via Hexham, Haydon Bridge, Alston and Penrith. (RS)

When the Passenger Transport Executives (PTEs) were created in the early 1970s, Midland Red relinquished a lot of its Birmingham area services to West Midlands' PTE. Shortly afterwards, Midland Red went on an acquisition spree and, as well as purchasing Cooper of Oakengates, they purchased the much larger business of Harper Bros of Heath Hayes. Formerly number 62 in the Harper's fleet, Duple Viceroy-bodied VAM70 FBF 794H became 2262 in the Midland Red fleet and soon received full NBC coach livery. (RS)

Yes, it is a VAM! Between 1982 and 1990, Mr E. L. Farrar of Fraddon in Cornwall built three bodies on Bedford chassis, all replicas of London General AEC double-decker buses. It is testament to his skills that all three are still running today, especially when the chassis are over fifty years old and the bodies over thirty. The one seen here is DFB704D, rebuilt as a replica of LGOC B1934 but originally fitted with a Duple body and new to Roman City of Bath. Going to school next to St Austell Brewery, I am very familiar with the ales listed on the advertising poster and, whilst the three buses are now spread out across England, in this view it had not strayed too far from home, being pictured outside the Great Western Hotel in Newquay. (MH)

The YRQ and YRT

By 1970, UK operators were expressing a level of dissatisfaction with the lack of development by lightweight chassis manufacturers, especially when compared to the advances made to heavyweights. The VAL and VAM were particularly criticised for their poor braking capabilities and interior noise levels, especially from that front-mounted engine situated inside the passenger saloon. Operators who preferred lightweight chassis were demanding that Ford and Bedford followed the lead of manufacturers such as AEC and Leyland, and put the engine anywhere but at the front. Not only would this improve noise level comfort for driver and passengers but if the engine were moved away from being vertically mounted at the front and mounted horizontally under the chassis, then the floor height of the body could be lowered, reducing the number of steps needed to get onto the vehicle in the first place. Whilst Ford remained with the front engine layout until the end of their PSV production, Bedford's answer arrived in 1970 with the 10-metre-long YRQ, fitted with the 7.6-litre Bedford 466 engine mounted centrally under the floor, and fitted with the same Turner gearbox as the VAM. Two years later it was joined by the 11-metre-long YRT, which received an Eaton gearbox, air brakes and power steering. For the home market, the YRQ and YRT were direct replacements for the VAM and VAL, and the YRQ chassis was essentially a modified VAM chassis. The 466 engine mounted amidships under the floor might have solved the access and noise problems, but it was still underpowered compared to the 11- and 12-litre offerings from other manufacturers. Only two years after the introduction of the YRQ plans were afoot to replace both it and the YRT with chassis with more powerful engines.

My first recollection of Tyne & Wear PTE's coaching arm, Armstrong Galley, was seeing the impressive MCW Metroliners operating the non-stop 'LONDONEWCASTLE Clipper' service during my days on National Express starting in the late 1980s. The name came about when the PTE acquired the businesses of R. Armstrong (Bus Proprietor) Ltd and Galley's Coaches Ltd in 1973. The Armstrong Galley name was used almost from day one of the take overs, so it is unusual to see just one name on a coach. Here is Galley's liveried 1972 Plaxton Panorama Elite YRQ BTY 729K in King's Cross, having brought Newcastle United supporters to London in 1974. (AS)

George Summerson commenced bus operations in 1927 with a fourteen-seat Chevrolet. He was later joined by his brother William, and the new business started using the fleet name 'The Eden'. In 1995 The Eden was acquired by United Automobile Services Ltd and became part of Arriva Group Plc. Seen in Bishop Auckland marketplace in 1974 is CPT 196L, a 1973 YRQ with Plaxton Derwent II body. (AS)

Seen standing above Edinburgh Waverley railway station is Edinburgh Corporation Transport's 243 (AFS 243K), one of only a handful of YRTs fitted with the Duple Viceroy body before Duple introduced the Dominant range. The demolition site behind was the old Waverley Market, which made way for the new shopping centre which now occupies the site. (AS)

In 1969, the well-known Leeds-based tour operator Wallace Arnold purchased London-based Woburn Garages, trading as Evan Evans, to give Wallace Arnold a foot into the Continental market. Evan Evans was never seen as a happy fit into the WA empire, and was finally sold in 1984. KUM 529L, a 1973 YRQ with Plaxton Panorama Elite III body, is seen departing from Fairfield Halls, Croydon in 1975. (AS)

I do like to include unique vehicles in my books, so here we see Hedingham Omnibus L81 (YNO 481L), a 1973 YRT fitted with a Marshall Camair body. Whilst the Camair was a rare beast, this was the only one built on a Bedford chassis. It was originally used as a demonstrator in full Hedingham livery, and so was acquired by the company at an 'advantageous' price. It subsequently passed to fellow Essex operator Partridge of Hadleigh but sadly burnt out in a fire at their yard in 1999. It is seen here in happier times at Sible Hedingham garage in 1975. (AS)

SELNEC (South East Lancashire, North East Cheshire) was the original name of the PTE formed on the 1 November 1969 to take over the Manchester area municipal operators, and whilst most of the 2500-plus-strong fleet were buses, a small number of coaches were operated. Eight Duple Viceroy-bodied YRQs were delivered in 1972, two of which, including 0040 (TNB 441K), were fitted with the Express version of the body, complete with folding entrance doors and destination blinds, primarily for use on the service between central Manchester and Ringway Airport (as Manchester Airport was then known). It is seen when new, passing what is now the Mercure hotel in Manchester's Piccadilly Gardens. (RS)

Caetano coachwork was becoming increasingly popular following its introduction to the UK in 1969, with well over 200 examples being delivered before Cascais-bodied YRQ OWY 338K arrived at Rossie Motors in 1972. It later passed to Beehive of Adwick-le-Street when Rossie's coaching activities were taken over in 1975. Seen here at Christ Church, Doncaster, it retains Rossie's green livery to which Beehive's fleet name and logo have been added. (RS)

Bedfords were the backbone of the Barton fleet for many years, and nearly every model of the chassis was operated before the final examples joined the fleet in 1981. They may have ordered their last actual VALs in 1964, but their first 11-metre Bedfords, a batch of ten fifty-three-seat Plaxton Panorama Elite-bodied YRTs, were also VALs, all carrying VAL registration plates! 1253 (VAL 966L) is seen two months after delivery, paintwork and wheeltrims gleaming as it waits at Heathrow Airport in 1973. (AS)

Back in the late 1970s, I was in the local junior St John Ambulance Brigade – something I joined on the insistence of a couple of school friends, completely unaware that I couldn't stand the sight of blood. Anyway, we went on a trip to the Forest of Dean to practice our cooking, cleaning, bandaging and fainting skills, and were transported from Bristol to the Forest in this very vehicle! Willowbrook 002 Expressway-bodied YRT EDD 715L was new in 1972 to Perrett of Shipton Oliffe, passing to Bevan Brothers of Soudley, trading as Soudley Valley Coaches. A quick chat with the driver allowed me a visit to their depot the next day to inspect the rest of the fleet – a much better option than giving mouth to mouth to a rubber doll. (RS)

The NBC favoured heavyweight chassis for their National Travel operations, specifically the Leyland Leopard, but that's not to say there wasn't a place for lighter-weight chassis as the following photographs show. Parked outside the York House Hotel on Eastbourne's Royal Parade, when brand new in April 1974, are Midland General's 76 and 77 (XRC 605/6M), two of the three Duple Dominant-bodied YRQs delivered that year, all three only seating forty-one to provide extra legroom for extended tour work. (AS)

If memory serves me correctly, the thirteen 002 Expressways delivered to South Wales Transport were the only examples of the model delivered new to the NBC. Fitted with coach seats, they were painted in dual-purpose local coach livery. Whilst the large panoramic windows were very passenger friendly, their size, combined with the thin body pillars, led to the Expressways having relatively short lives due to the lack of structural integrity. 219 (PWN 219M) was a YRQ delivered in 1974 and is seen in Gloucester bus station on a National Travel service to Pembroke Dock. (RS)

By the mid-1970s, NBC was keen to rid itself of the assorted collection of vehicles it had inherited and move towards a more standardised fleet. The problem was supply of the Leyland National, NBC's new 'standard' single decker, was unable to keep up with demand. This resulted in batches of relatively cheap lightweight buses being purchased. Willowbrook bodied sixty YRQ and YRT chassis for United Counties. YRTs 115 and 119 (RBD 115M and TBD 619N) are seen in their hometown bus station of Bedford. Delivered in 1974, and withdrawn only seven years later, they were quickly snapped up by independent operators across the UK. (AS)

Despite the Leyland Leopard being the preferred chassis for coachwork, Bedfords were still entering the National Travel fleets up until 1980, but their operating lives were much shorter than their heavyweight counterparts. Duple Dominant-bodied YRT VYM 507M was delivered to National Travel (South East) in 1973, but less than four years later had passed to Windsorian of Windsor and is seen passing Churchill's statue in Parliament Square, Westminster, in 1977. (AS)

Jollys of South Hylton commenced operating a service into Sunderland in 1923 and, following the closure of the railway, became a lifeline for the people of the area. Sadly, Jollys closed their doors in 1995 when the opening of the Tyne & Wear Metro made operations economically unviable. The fleet was almost 100 per cent Bedford, the majority being service buses all bought new, and one of Jolly's trademarks was to have seats fitted with slatted wooden bases, long after such items had been ruled ordinarily obsolete. Seen on Park Lane, Sunderland, on its first day in service in September 1974, is Willowbrook-bodied YRT PGR 619N, one of two put into service that day. (AS)

Following its success with Caetano bodies, Moseley's attempted to introduce the products of Finnish bodybuilder Lahden Autokori. Only two examples were imported, both on YRQ chassis, SYD 86M delivered to Arleen of Peasedown St John, Bath, and (seen here) GKM 406N new to Sonners of Gillingham in Kent. Records fail to say why it wasn't a success, as the body is very attractive, with more than a hint of Mercedes Benz 0302 about it. A second attempt to crack the UK market had more modest luck in recent years, thanks to its collaboration with Scania and production of the OmniExpress. However, it was that very collaboration that led to the bankruptcy of Lahden Autokori in 2011. (AS).

Skill's of Nottingham celebrated its centenary in 2019, having been founded in 1919 by Arthur Skill. The company is still family owned and operates an impressive fleet of top-spec coaches, and whilst Volvo, Scania and Setra now dominate the fleet, nearly eighty Bedfords were operated over the years. Amongst the last to be delivered was 57 (JAL 257N), a 1975 YRT with Plaxton Panorama Elite Express body (Skill's operated several express services to holiday destinations, and the coach is seen at Princes Park coach station in Eastbourne when two weeks old). (AS)

The Willowbrook 008 Spacecar, affectionately known as 'the plastic pig', may have looked futuristic at the time but its build quality was pretty appalling. Seen in front of the Davies Turner freight warehouse, at Battersea Wharf coach park, are three YRTs from the National Travel London fleet – JMY 123/1/2N – all delivered in 1975 and seen only four years later after withdrawal, with 122 appearing to have been in the wars more than the other two. (AS)

New to Douglas Corporation Transport in 1974, Willowbrook-bodied YRQ 18 (MAN 138B) was the penultimate new bus to be delivered to the corporation before it was merged with the Isle of Man Road Services company to form Isle of Man National Transport Limited in 1976. It is seen shortly before the merger in Douglas bus station. (AS)

Essex was once graced by numerous fascinating independents, including G.W. Osborne and Sons, based in the lovely village of Tollesbury. They operated a network of services across Essex, and for many years purchased batches of buses from London Transport, as well as demonstrators from AEC. One vehicle delivered new to the company, and in fact the last new service bus to be delivered, was Willowbrook-bodied YRT 20 (JEV 706N) seen here in Tollesbury Square. Osborne's was taken over by Hedingham Omnibuses in 1997, long after JEV had left the fleet. (AS)

An unusual purchase for a municipality was Caetano-bodied YRT JFW 184N, delivered to City of Lincoln in 1975. It was fitted with a toilet; a convenience (pardon the pun) that we accept as the norm on coaches nowadays but was considered such a selling point back in 1975 that Lincoln produced an A4 leaflet to advertise the luxury features of the coach, the intention being to promote Continental work. Unfortunately, the venture wasn't the success Lincoln hoped it would be and the coach was sold less than two years later. (AS)

GSX 121N was one of ten coach-seated Alexander 'Y Type'-bodied YRTs delivered new to Edinburgh Corporation Transport in 1975. They arrived painted in the black and white tour livery, but shortly after were repainted into madder and white. As a result of the Local Government (Scotland) Act of 1973, ownership of Edinburgh Corporation Transport passed to Lothian Regional Council's Department of Public Transport, and two months after GSX was delivered the operation was renamed Lothian Regional Transport. GSX 121N was withdrawn from service in 1982 after only seven years work but is still active today, having been bought for preservation in 2002. (AS)

The orange and maroon fleet of House's Watlington Buses contained no buses at all, only coaches, most of which were used to operate their stage carriage services across South Oxfordshire and North Berkshire. SJO 400N was a Duple Dominant-bodied YRQ new in 1975 and is seen outside Reading railway station. House's are no more, the company having ceased trading in 1987. However, the last new coach delivered to the company is now preserved in the Oxford Bus Museum. (AS)

I just had to include this picture of Market Drayton as it's where I live (well very nearly) and I can't believe how much it's changed! William's Garage has gone, although there is still a garage and car sales on the site. The bus shelter has also gone, replaced by a bus station which occupies the site where the market stall is. NCB Motors, the owner of Plaxton Panorama Elite-bodied YRQ JJU 462N, are no more, having been taken over by Lakeside of Ellesmere in 2019. The presence of the market stall means it must be a Wednesday, the only day that Drayton gets coach parties nowadays. (MH)

Another 'Y Type'-bodied YRT from north of the border is Eastern Scottish C746K (MSF 746P). Like many of the SBG subsidiaries, Eastern Scottish used codes to identify vehicle makes and depot allocations, C being the chassis code for Bedford, and K the depot code for Peebles, where the bus is seen in 1976. (AS)

As mentioned earlier, the United Counties Willowbrook-bodied Bedfords were quickly snapped up by independent operators across the UK when they were withdrawn. Cornish operator Grenville of Troon purchased two to supplement their fleet of similar vehicles, several of which came from other fleets featured in this book. LVV 125P is seen on a rather dismal day in Redruth (and having spent many years there, I can confirm that Redruth is pretty dismal) in the company of Duple Viceroy-bodied VAL XAW 550K, operated by Trelawney Tours of Hayle. (RS)

Yes, it really is an E registered Plaxton Panorama Elite-bodied YRT! Built in 1973 and delivered to Cleckheaton-based dealer Jack Hughes, it was one of several vehicles which remained unsold and were discovered when Mr Hughes passed away in 1987. It was bought, together with two similarly bodied coaches (one Bedford, one Ford), by Bob Smith Travel of Langley Park, and all three were registered for the first time, hence the E-prefix registration. It is seen in 1994 making its way up Waingate into Sheffield city centre, when owned by Serene Travel of Bedlington. It is interesting to note that it entered service just over a year after Bedford pulled out of the PSV market. (RS)

No, I've not gone mad; this is a Wright Contour (introduced in 1982) on a YRT (discontinued in 1977). Wrights of Ballymena may now be a big player in the UK bus market, but in the early 1980s they were better known for building rather utilitarian-looking buses, usually for the welfare market. Then, in 1982, after working with General Motors' styling department, they introduced the Contour. With its graceful swooping lines and (optional) spats on the rear wheels, it was completely leftfield for Wrights, and whilst most were built on new Bedford chassis, SKG 811M had its Duple Dominant body replaced with a Contour in 1984 at the behest of owners Beeline of Warminster. (AS)

The YLQ and YMT

For years, Bedfords had been seen as being 'cheap and cheerful'; perfect vehicles for trundling round the cabbage patch, but not really suitable for the long haul. But times were changing, and with the decline of the railway network and increase in motorway mileage, more and more operators were looking to literally go that extra mile and add destinations further from home into their day excursion brochures. Whilst the introduction of the 466 engine was seen as significant for Bedford, it wasn't ideal for getting to those far afield places as quickly as people wanted, and with motorway speed limits for PSVs set at 70 mph, something more was needed than a coach that was happy plodding away at 55 mph, especially when the heavyweight chassis manufacturers were now using engines of 11- and 12-litre capacity. The answer came in the shape of the Detroit-designed 8.2-litre 500 series, first seen in the UK at the 1972 Commercial Motor Show. The engine first appeared in a Bedford coach two years later rated at 138 bhp when the 10-metre-long YLQ replaced the YRQ and shortly afterwards the YRT was replaced by the YMT, the engine in the 11-metre chassis being uprated to 157 bhp. Both the YLQ and YMT continued to use the Eaton five-speed gearbox as used in the YRT.

Things should now have been going well for Bedford – new more powerful engines enabling coaches to cruise at higher speeds – however the PSV market was changing. One factor was rising unemployment that meant fewer people needed taking to and from work and fewer could afford to travel for leisure. Another was that the independent sector, where Bedford took most of its business from, was taking a greater interest in high-specification coaches, whose additional on-board features resulted in higher body weights, which in many cases saw the body weight exceeding the maximum permitted gross weight for the Bedford chassis. Operators had also found that whilst a heavyweight chassis might initially cost more, they were more suited to high-speed running than Bedfords, and this increased reliability worked out favourably against the initial extra outlay. The YLQ and YMT were also prone to suffering from engine failures caused mostly by proprietary components such as oil and water pumps. Water pump failures quite often led to the fan shearing off and slicing through the radiator. Whilst plans were put in place to address these issues, they didn't happen quickly enough, and Bedford's reputation started to slide.

Seen outside Rye railway station in 1988 is Fuggles of Benenden's Duple Dominant bus-bodied YLQ NKE 303P. Judging by the wet oil around the engine flap, either the engine is gassing or someone hasn't replaced the dipstick or oil filler cap properly. Interesting information on the yellow noticeboard announcing a new car park for British Rail and bus garage for Hastings & District. (MH)

As I commenced writing this book it was announced that long-established Kenzie's Coaches would be closing following the retirement of owner Cyril Kenzie, and some of the fleet of immaculately preserved Bedfords have already passed into new hands. New to Kenzie's in 1976, and still sporting their livery, is Duple Dominant-bodied YLQ LER 666P, seen arriving at Springfields in Spalding in the ownership of Camelot Coaches. (RS)

From the Corvedale Coaches arm of the Whittle Group is 46 (RAW 46R), one of fifteen Duple Dominant II-bodied YLQs delivered in 1976. It is seen at Princes Park coach park in Eastbourne in 1978. The 'On Hire to Southdown' board in the window indicates a practice commonly used (by visiting tour coaches across Britain) in the days before deregulation to allow them to do day trips for their passengers without having to apply for their own excursion licence. (AS)

Number B30 in the fleet of Gash of Newark was this 1976 Plaxton Supreme-bodied YLQ RAU 624R. It is seen entering Newark bus station having suffered a minor front-end altercation. In 1989 it passed just down the road to the fleet of Marshalls of Sutton on Trent, and after further use it went into store for many years with the intention of preserving it. Unfortunately, it was found to be beyond economic repair and was scrapped in 2013. (RS)

I've included this line-up of coaches in South Yorkshire PTE's Doncaster Leicester Avenue depot to show the evolution of Plaxton's body range. All were owned by the PTE but carry different liveries. Lined up in order of age: 1014 (EWY 590C) is a 1965 Plaxton Panorama-bodied AEC Reliance in Travel Line livery, 1021 (PWE 714K), a 1972 Reliance with Plaxton Panorama Elite Express body in Booth & Fisher livery, and finally 1098 (PKY 418R), a 1977 Plaxton Supreme-bodied YLQ acquired from Blue Ensign and still carrying their livery. (RS)

A closer look at PKY 418R, the former Blue Ensign YLQ, by now carrying full SYPTE livery. Caught on camera in Preston bus station after taking competitors to a Taekwondo competition in the nearby Guild Hall. Its two compatriots also had a SYPTE link. Premier of Stainforth's Ford FCX 579W would become number 89 in the SYPTE fleet when the PTE acquired Premier, whilst Caetano Estoril-bodied Ford SDT 918L on the far right was new to Doncaster Corporation, and became part of the SYPTE fleet before being sold to Buckley's of Doncaster. (RS)

New to Hills of Tredegar as RBO 673R, Plaxton Supreme Express-bodied YLQ 865 YET had received a Supreme IV front when caught parked in Plymouth Bretonside bus station, in 1990, in the ownership of Robins' Travel of Ford, near Chippenham. It is surrounded by coaches I grew up with; one of Kinsman of Bodmin's Caetano Alpha-bodied Fords to the left, Fry's of Tintagel's Plaxton Supreme V-bodied YNT NGL 491X behind, and a Plaxton Paramount-bodied Volvo of Plymouth City Coach above. (PG)

Formed in 1913, Applebys were one of the largest operators in Lincolnshire and, despite being taken over by the Bowen Group in 2000, sadly failed to make the magic century of operating, Bowen's entering receivership in 2012. Seen on service in Bridlington is Plaxton Supreme-bodied YLQ VAT 176S, new to Boddy's of Bridlington in 1977. (RS)

The Maltby Miners Transport and Home Coal Delivery Service existed to deliver miners' allocations of free coal, but also operated a local bus service between Maltby and Maltby Colliery, the timetable of which was designed to meet the miners' shift changes. The fleet included Willowbrook-bodied YRQ NET 888M and YLQ THE 50S, both purchased new and seen attending a Miners Gala at Doncaster Racecourse. (RS)

Another star of stage and screen was Duple Dominant II-bodied YLQ/S CYH 797V, from the Grey Green fleet, as in 1981 it appeared in an episode of the children's TV drama *Grange Hill*, going on an aborted school trip to France. Closer to home and having made it to its destination this time, it is seen arriving at Wembley Stadium in 1984. (AS)

Davies Brothers of Pencader was formed in 1926, initially running a service from Carmarthen to Lampeter. It remained a family business, growing to become one of Wales' biggest independent operators, with a network of services across south and west Wales. In the later years of operation Bedfords were the preferred choice for new vehicles. Duple Dominant bus-bodied YLQ WBX 7T is seen leaving Carmarthen on the Lampeter service. (RS)

Many ex-UK Bedfords ended their lives in Malta, some being extensively re-engineered. Just because it said Bedford on the front didn't mean it hadn't received an engine from something else. However, in this case the only alterations are the top sliding side windows and bus seats. Plaxton Supreme-bodied YLQ EBY-477 was originally YRY 509T and was new to Lesters of Long Whatton, but as shown on the front nameplate had also operated with Boyden's of Castle Donington. New in 1978, it arrived in Malta in 1986. (RS)

The small Nottinghamshire village of Dunham-on-Trent was home to Brumpton's Coachways. Between 1950 and 1983, every vehicle purchased new was a Bedford, fitted with either Plaxton or Duple coachwork. Delivered in 1979 was this immaculate Plaxton Supreme-bodied YLQ GCH 985V, seen parked in Scarborough without a Continental interloper in sight. (RS)

FBX 561W was one of three Duple Dominant bus-bodied YLQs purchased by Davies Bros in 1981, and despite being 10 metres long managed to seat fifty passengers by use of 3 + 2 seating towards the rear. Unusually, the buses were fitted with Allison fully automatic gearboxes. After sale by Davies, they moved to the north of the country and joined the fleet of E. Jones of Ponciau near Wrexham. (AS)

Let's finish this chapter with something that isn't quite what it seems. Despite having a 1980 registration, the YLQ chassis on MGS 437V dates from 1976 and the Alexander 'Y' type body from 1973. The body was originally fitted to WXE 264M, a Bedford YRQ demonstrator, and was later removed and fitted onto an unregistered YLQ chassis and used as a test bed for the YMP. (PG)

At first glance a standard Duple Dominant, however closer inspection reveals that it's slightly higher. This is JKX 742N, the original Duple Goldliner, a Vauxhall Motors demonstrator built in 1975 as the prototype YMT. It was fitted with an experimental Bedford 500 turbo engine and, although seen here in National livery at the 1976 Brighton Coach Rally, was later lent to Tricentrol of Dunstable for testing on behalf of Bedford. As well as testing at home, the coach was also sent to rather more exotic locations, including Morocco for heat testing. (AS)

With Bedford obviously keen to make the YMT a success, it was important the new chassis was seen in some of the UK's major fleets. One of the first YMTs off the production line in 1976 was Duple Dominant-bodied NNW 116P, delivered to Wallace Arnold's Leeds fleet. However, it was a case of odd man out as no further YMTs were ordered by WA. It is seen departing from Croydon in 1978 on what was hopefully the first pick-up on the tour to 'Beautiful' Scarborough. (AS)

The lack of orders from Wallace Arnold was more than made up for by those placed by the Ewer Group, who standardised on the Duple Dominant-bodied YMT for many years. Their first order was in 1976 for thirteen for the Grey Green fleet, and MUL 697P is seen arriving at Princes Park in Eastbourne, so new that it had still not received its destination blind. (AS)

In 1977, Duple replaced the Dominant with the Dominant II, which had a deeper windscreen and less fussy front end. Amongst the first delivered to the NBC were five YMTs for the National Travel subsidiary Greenslades. 379 (STA 379R) is seen at the top of Beachy Head, near Eastbourne, in 1978, awaiting the return of its tour passengers to collect their packed lunches. (AS)

Roman City of Bath was one of the area's largest independent coach operators and was amongst the first to undertake guided coach tours of Bath. The company was purchased by Badgerline in the early days of deregulation, with the intention of operating Roman City as a separate private hire division, but after a few years the name was quietly dropped. Plaxton Supreme-bodied YMT OHT 864R was delivered new in 1977 and is seen waiting on the forecourt of Bath Spa railway station. Love that little Ford Fiesta Supersport in the background. (AS)

As mentioned in the main text, Tricentrol of Dunstable carried out a Bedford-approved conversion on the YMT to extend it to 12 metres in length. RGS 598R was the first one to be completed and, after being fitted with a fifty-seven-seat Duple Dominant II body, entered service with Tricentrol's own coach fleet in 1977. It is seen here at the side of St Mark's bus station in Lincoln after having passed to Eagre of Gainsborough. (RS)

In the mid-1970s, the Ewer Group went on an acquisition spree, buying Dix of Dagenham outright and taking a controlling interest in World Wide of Camberwell. Both fleets had very different vehicle buying policies, with Dix preferring Fords, and World Wide favouring AEC and Mercedes. Whilst World Wide received five Dominant II-bodied YMTs in 1977, the Dix fleet continued to receive new Fords, but eventually came into line with the rest of the group. The individual Ewer Group fleets retained their own separate identities and liveries, and vehicles were ordered with their recipient fleet in mind, ensuring that the seats matched the exterior livery: blue for World Wide, as seen on RYL 705R, and orange and brown for Dix, as seen on VYU 759S. (AS)

Second-hand vehicles rarely found their way into NBC fleets, but one such coach was Duple Dominant YMT SVJ 300S, which became number 846 in the Midland Red West fleet. It was new to Yeomans of Canon Pyon and was acquired when Midland Red bought Yeomans' Hereford to London service to stop it competing with National Express' own service. Rather ironic that nowadays Yeomans operate the Hereford to London service on behalf of National Express. It is seen turning onto Buckingham Palace Road ready to pull into London Victoria coach station, the lack of full NBC-style destination equipment showing it was a non-standard coach in the fleet. (AS)

In the early 1980s, quite a few original Plaxton Supremes (and some Panorama Elites) received the more modern Supreme IV front end, but not many received the more modern Paramount front end. The difference in windscreen depths is evident by the pronounced drop between the bottom of the side windows and windscreen. YMT VWK 7S was new to Harry Shaw of Coventry in 1977 and passed to Rambler of Hastings when just a year old. In 1989 it received its front-end transplant and accrued a creditable nineteen years' service before it was burnt out in 1996. (AS)

Deregulation of Britain's buses in 1986 saw operators rush to register local bus services, resulting in a requirement for suitable vehicles. Willowbrook introduced the rather angular Warrior, with all but one being a rebody on older chassis, in some cases replacing coach bodies such as Willowbrook's own 008 Spacecar. YMT XNM 830S, however, was originally fitted with a Van Hool McArdle body, and was delivered new to Armchair of Brentford. After receiving its Warrior body in 1986, it passed to West Midlands independent Cave of Shirley and is seen in Solihull town centre. (AS)

By pure coincidence, the subject of this photo also received a Warrior body. Duple Dominant II-bodied YMT TER 5S was new to Kenzie's of Shepreth in 1978. It passed to Maidstone Borough Council to operate the rather random City Flyer service between Dover and Blackpool via London, Leicester, Sheffield and Halifax, operated jointly with Leicester City Transport and Burnley & Pendle. When the service (which end to end must have been quite an ordeal in a YMT) ended in 1989, Maidstone sent the coach to Willowbrook where it received its Warrior body. (RS)

Mainstream imports of Belgian-built Van Hool bodies began with the Vistadome in the early 1970s, before moving on to the 300 Line in 1975. Nearly 300 of the 300 Line were actually built in Dublin, Van Hool having taken over the bodybuilding factory of Irish National Transport Company (CIE) in 1971 to form Van Hool-McArdle. Entered in the 1978 Brighton Coach Rally was YMT TPJ 272S of Banstead Coaches, and whilst there was no silverware that year, the following year Dudley Haynes of Banstead Coaches was to become Coach Driver of the Year. (AS)

We've seen several constituents of the Ewer Group so we might as well see one more! The long-established firm of Orange Luxury Coaches of Brixton was acquired in 1953, together with the ornately fronted coach station in Effra Road, Brixton, which, when built in 1927, was the first motor coach station in London. It remained as a separate subsidiary of Grey Green until wound up in December 1975. However, coaches continued to wear the Orange livery name and, more importantly, the Queen's Arms, as Orange was supplier of coaches to the royal household. Dominant II-bodied YMT TYE 702S is seen in Parliament Square when new in 1978. (AS)

East meets West ... in Sheffield. One of the aims of the NBC was to achieve some form of vehicular standardisation across the fleet. To an extent this was achieved quite quickly within the National Travel division as, by the late 1970s, all coaches were bodied by Willowbrook, Duple or Plaxton. Dominant II-bodied YMT OKY 80R from National Travel East is en route to Leeds, whilst Plaxton Supreme-bodied YUE 600S from National Travel West is making its way to Wolverhampton. (RS)

In 1979, Moseley's were at it again, this time as UK concessionaires for Spanish bodybuilder Union Carrocera, or Unicar. In the three years the Unicar GT80 body was imported, just over 100 entered service, mostly on YMTs, but with some Volvo B58s and a solitary Ford. The GT80 was launched by Moseley's at the 1979 Brighton Coach Rally, where DFJ 324T, the prototype, was displayed in the livery of Hookway's of Meeth, Devon. (AS)

Eastern National's 1215 (BNO 701T) was one of eighteen Duple Dominant II-bodied YMTs delivered in 1978/9 to operate the company's longer distance stage services, hence the fitment of express doors and painting in local coach livery. It is seen approaching London Victoria coach station in 1979 on the 084 service from Walton-on-the-Naze. When I joined Wessex coaches in 1995, we had a small outstation in Walton specifically to operate the 084, now running as a National Express service. (AS)

I always remember the Morecambe and Wise joke where Ernie asks 'who's Googie Withers' and Eric replying, 'everyone's does in winter'. Plaxton Supreme IV-bodied EWF 209V was operated by Peter Withers of Barnby Dun in the livery of previous owner Larratt Pepper of Thurnscoe. Larratt Pepper operated a small fleet of immaculate Bedfords, such as the one I was allocated when working for Sanders of Holt. We bought it in 1994; it was twelve years old at the time and didn't have a blemish on it. (RS)

Caetano's replacement for the Estoril/Cascais/Lisboa range arrived in the UK in 1978 in the shape of the rather angular Alpha. Red Rover FJO 144V was one of ten YMTs bought between 1978 and 1980, six of which were fitted with Caetano bodies. They were among the last coaches purchased by Red Rover before the company disbanded its coaching arm to concentrate solely on local bus work. (RS)

Formed in 1921, Felix of Stanley's name came from a popular song of the day, 'Felix Kept on Walking', and the black cat image was used by the company until 2009. Early that year, a large American company, Felix the Cat Creations Inc., advised Felix that it owned the copyright to all images of cats used next to the Felix name, and unable to afford to fight a court case, Felix removed the image from their vehicles. Duple Dominant II-bodied YMT BRR 684T is seen in 1981 in Derby bus station operating Felix's core route to Ilkeston. (RS)

Van Hool's Aragon body became available in the UK in 1979 and introduced styling that would continue through into the Alizee; the body which would really bring Van Hool to the forefront of UK coaching. Armchair of Brentford were one of the first operators of Van Hools in the UK, taking a pair of Seddons in 1971, as well as several 300 Lines, so it was natural that they would be one of the first to take delivery of an Aragon. YMT HRO 430V is seen on Madeira Drive, Brighton, in 1980. (AS)

Same fleet; different colours. Following local government reorganisation in 1974, Maidstone Corporation Transport became Maidstone Borough Council Transport. The buses retained the pale blue and cream corporation livery, but in 1979, to commemorate the seventy-fifth anniversary of municipal transport in Maidstone, the ochre colour scheme previously used by Maidstone Corporation on its trolleybuses was painted onto a single decker, this later becoming the standard livery. Wadham Stringer Vanguard II-bodied YMT 183 (MKP 183W) leads yet to be repainted Duple Dominant bus-bodied YMT 165 (WKE 65S). (RS)

It seems almost inconceivable nowadays that, until relatively recently, factories operated their own buses for staff transport, but this was a regular scene outside the Austin Reed/Chester Barrie factory in Crewe. Plaxton Supreme IV-bodied YMT HUH 996W was new to Evans Coaches of Senghenydd, South Wales, and after service at the clothing factory returned to PSV operation with Kidsgrove-based Stanways Coaches. The Duple Dominant-bodied YRT was new to National Travel North East as JKU 457P before moving to Tours (Isle of Man) as T111 MAN, receiving RMA 609P on its return to the mainland. (MH)

Probably the most south-westerly coach operator in Britain is Mounts Bay Coaches of Marazion in Cornwall, so named because their depot overlooks St Michael's Mount on the outskirts of Penzance. New to Rutherford of London as EMJ 991T is Plaxton Supreme IV-bodied YMT MIB 9068. The eagle-eyed amongst you will have spotted the Cummins lettering on the front grille, denoting that the coach is fitted with the 5.9-litre Cummins 6BTA engine. Whilst the 160 bhp produced by the standard Bedford 500 engine might have been adequate for some operators, those wanting to get that bit of extra 'oomph' found that the Cummins unit fitted the bill perfectly and was a relatively easy conversion to undertake. (PG)

In 1981, Duple replaced the Dominant II with the Dominant III and IV, and whilst the IV had conventional windows, those on the III were trapezoid shaped as seen here. Whether the designer was trying to emulate the American Greyhound Scenicruiser coaches I don't know, but from a passenger's point of view they were a disaster – the thickness of the side pillars meant that some seats had a severely restricted view. Before moving into local bus work, Leicestershire-based GK Kinch operated a high-quality coach fleet, including YMT PAY 5W, seen unloading in Moreton-in-Marsh. (RS)

Tricentrol built up a sizeable coaching fleet in quite a short space of time by taking over established firms including Bunty Costin of Dunstable, Travel House of Luton, Buckmaster of Leighton Buzzard, North Star of Stevenage, Howletts of Quorn, Housden-Caldwell of Loughborough and Halls Silverline of Hounslow. By the mid-1980s the group had started to split, and in 1988 the last pieces were sold to Luton & District. Seen in Victoria coach station in 1981 is Duple Dominant III-bodied YMT UMJ 420W. (AS)

Willowbrook's final big foray was with the dual-purpose 003, nearly all of which were fitted to Leyland Leopards for NBC subsidiaries. Four were ordered by independent operators, including this one-off for Excelsior of Dinnington. New in 1981, YMT LHE 334W was fitted with a deeper windscreen than previous examples and round headlights, as well as being kitted out to full executive-spec, with forty-four seats, toilet and video. It is seen on Epsom Downs on Derby Day in 1981, two months after delivery but sadly was written off on the Continent just a few weeks after this picture was taken. (RS)

NBC also received some YMQ/S Tricentrol conversions, all bodied by companies not usually associated with the nationalised operation. Ten examples, fitted with thirty-three-seat dual-purpose Wadham Stringer Vanguard bodies, were delivered to Eastern National in 1980. They were a very attractive little bus and looked very well proportioned. 1052 (TJN 978W) is seen on Enfield Broadway in 1986. (AS)

When tendering of London Transport routes commenced, Eastern National was quick to take advantage and won the W9 from Enfield to Muswell Hill Broadway on the first tender round in 1985. The W9 was one of LT's first minibus routes, using Strachan-bodied Ford Transits. Eastern National branded the route the 'W-Niner', with the buses based at Ponders End, hence the PD depot plate on YMQ/S 1052 (TJN 975W), seen travelling down Church Street in Enfield. (AS)

The two-tone green coaches of Harris of Grays were a familiar sight across the Continent and, when bus services were deregulated in 1986, Harris Bus was established, gaining contracts in Essex and, from 1997, in London. An early transfer from the coach to bus fleet was twenty-eight-seat Plaxton Supreme IV-bodied YMQ RWC 651W, which had been converted to 8-metre length by Tricentrol. If you look carefully you can just make out that the coach is fitted with manual Setright ticket machine and cash tray. (AS)

Another Tricentrol conversion was Plaxton Supreme IV-bodied YMQ UUR 341W, new to Armchair of Brentford. It is seen on layover in Yeovil bus station in the ownership of Wake's of Sparkford, its trademark Armchair orange seats having been retrimmed sometime in its life. (MH)

The penultimate Bedford supplied new to Kenzie's of Shepreth was 1981 Plaxton Supreme IV-bodied YMQ HFL 14W, seen awaiting its afternoon school run in 2006. Such was the high standard of the Kenzie's fleet, the nigh on forty-year-old remained in use with Kenzie's until the end of operations in 2019. (PG)

The rest of the NBC YMQ/Ss were fitted with rather angular Lex Maxeta bodies, five for South Wales Transport, to replace the last of the AEC Regent Vs on the Pennard route, and three for United Counties. From the SWT batch, LCY 302X (along with one of the United Counties examples) passed to Buffalo of Flitwick and was re-registered 7178 KP. Buffalo branched out into bus work after deregulation before being sold to Arriva The Shires in 1995. It is seen here on St Peter's Street in St Albans. (AS)

Despite the introduction of the YNT in 1980 and Venturer in 1985, YMT production continued until 1987, primarily to operators wanting a non-turbo, steel-sprung chassis for local service work, like Duple Dominant bus-bodied C668 WRT, delivered to Chambers of Bures in 1986. Chambers purchased their first bus in 1918 to operate a service between Sudbury and Colchester and, when the company was sold to Go-Ahead in 2012, operated twenty-seven buses on a network of services across Essex and Suffolk. (AS)

Whilst Duple's Dominant bus looked nothing like its coaching counterpart, Plaxton's Derwent 300 had a passing family resemblance to the Paramount range it ran alongside. Introduced in 1986, it was the second Plaxton bus body to be named after the Derbyshire River, the previous one being discontinued in 1977 when Plaxton paused building bus bodies. Following deregulation, Epsom Coaches entered the local bus market with Epsom Buses, and in 1987 purchased five Derwent-bodied YMTs, (some of the last to enter service) including newly delivered D603 RGJ, seen outside Epsom railway station in January of that year. (AS)

Jesse Dell formed Rover Bus Service in Chesham in 1928, his son, John, subsequently taking over the running of the company, a position he held until the company closed in 1999 following John Dell's retirement. For many years they operated a service between Chesham and Hemel Hempstead using mainly Bedfords and Fords, and Plaxton Derwent 3000-bodied YMT D620 PWA was the last new Bedford purchased by the company. It is seen on London Road in Hemel Hempstead in 1988. (AS)

The roots of Metrobus go back to 1981 when Tillingbourne of Cranleigh took over the operations of Orpington & District, setting up a new company, Tillingbourne (Metropolitan) Ltd. In 1983, two of Tillingbourne's directors took over the subsidiary and renamed it Metrobus, initially operating three routes around Croydon. D22 CTR was one of three Wadham Stringer Vanguard-bodied YMTs purchased in 1986 to operate LRT tendered services including the 357 from Croydon to Orpington. (AS)

Enter the Turbo

The deregulation of the UK coaching industry saw a huge rise in the number of operators keen to send vehicles 'over the water', either on shuttles to the south of France or Spain or increasing their Continental tour programme. It came as no surprise to see more and more Continental manufacturers selling their wares into UK operators, and the likes of Volvo, Scania and DAF started to make huge inroads into UK fleets. With their air-sprung chassis and powerful smooth turbocharged engines, it made perfect sense for operators using the Continent to buy coaches manufactured there, especially when mechanical back-up was required. Bedford, realising that this was the way the market was heading, looked to improve both power and reliability, and in 1981 introduced a turbocharger to the 500 series engines. Rated at 205 bhp, it was initially the only engine available in Bedford's new flagship chassis, the YNT. Fitted with a six-speed gearbox initially, the Turner M6 proved to be problematic and so was replaced with the ZF S6-65; the YNT really did bring Bedford into the motorway cruising league.

The combination of the more powerful engine, combined with a higher-geared rear axle, meant that the YNT's mechanical set-up was a much better proposition for engine life and reliability. Despite it still being a steel-sprung chassis, the YNT was to remain in production until the end of Bedford PSV chassis, the last one being delivered in 1988. The naturally aspirated 500 engine was subsequently made available in the YNT to satisfy operators who wanted the new chassis with its six-speed gearbox, but didn't require the extra power of the turbocharged engine. Whilst the turbocharged engine was offered as an option in new YMTs, being just over an inch taller than the naturally aspirated version, it wasn't suitable for retrofitting into older vehicles. A derated version was fitted to the YLQ, changing its chassis designation initially to YMQ, and then when the powerplant was uprated, it became the YMP. I can confirm that these models (especially when shortened to become the 8-metre-long YMP/S) were real flying machines!

The first production YNTs arrived in the early part of 1981 on 'W' suffix registration plates, one of the first being Plaxton Supreme IV-bodied ORC 416W delivered to Rainworth Travel of Langwith. It is seen here loading in Hardy Street, Worksop, whilst on service to Ollerton with what looks like Jim MacDonald from Coronation Street waiting to get on. (RS)

To operate their service to Durham, Gypsy Queen of Langley Park would buy brand-new Bedfords with express door coach bodies and replace the coach seats with bus seats, carefully storing the coach seats away. When the coaches were sold (usually after only two years) the seats were swapped back, resulting in a nearly new coach with a brand-new set of seats. Seen in Durham, YNT KTY 426X is fitted with a rare express version of the Dominant III complete with PAYE sign fitted into the front grille. (RS)

For the 1982 season, Plaxton introduced the Supreme V and VI models, the main difference from the Supreme IV being the more upright rear end with large flat rear window and rectangular light clusters. Amongst the first YNTs to receive the Supreme V was a batch of nine delivered to Clarkes of London, all fitted with express doors, not for undertaking service work, but to speed up loading tourists in London. BGS 293X later passed to Minerva Travel of Melksham and is seen here in Chippenham operating Wiltshire Council Service 33 to Devizes. (RS)

New to Waterhouse of Polegate in 1982 as TPN 750X is this Plaxton Supreme VI-bodied YNT. The shallow side windows are clearly evident, and whilst of a similar height to Duple's Dominant III, their conventional layout allowed an unrestricted view for passengers. This version of the Supreme VI was badged as the 'Jubilee Supreme VI GT', as it was launched in Plaxton's seventy-fifth year and was fitted with a rear-mounted toilet. It is seen here still wearing Waterhouse's livery with subsequent owner Smiths of Corby Glen in Lincolnshire turning into the coach park at Wembley. (AS)

Well I can honestly say I've never typed 'Castrosua Brisa 300' before – probably because there was only one such vehicle bodied by the Spanish company for the UK market. YNT KGA 87Y was imported by Moseley's in 1982 and delivered to Nationwide of Lanark, and as seen here later passing to Terry Field of Doncaster. (RS)

Hornsby's of Ashby have provided local bus services to the people of Scunthorpe and the surrounding areas for over 100 years using an immaculately presented fleet of vehicles. Whilst a fleet of buses is used on stage carriage work these days, coaches were used in the past. Seen departing Scunthorpe bus station is Duple Dominant IV-bodied YNT HBH 411Y, one of a pair new to Arrowline of West Drayton in 1983. (RS)

Another vehicle with an HBH/Y registration is very early Plaxton Paramount 3200-bodied YNT HBH 418Y, seen here parked in Skegness in the ownership of Goodfellow of Wadsley Bridge. Introduced for the 1983 season, the Paramount was the successor to the long-running Supreme and was initially available in two heights, the 3200 and 3500, both indicating the vehicles height in millimetres. (RS)

Duple Dominant bus-bodied YNT OBX 453Y had been new in 1983 to Davies of Pencader, but is seen here on layover in Northampton with Buckby's Coaches of Rothwell. It was a remarkable survivor, still being in service with the company in the mid-2000s when well over twenty years old. Buckby's commenced operations in the early 1920s and even through the company has been through several changes of owner, the name is still in use today. (RS)

Established in 1915, St Dunstan's (now known as Blind Veterans UK) is a charity providing free support and services to vision-impaired ex-Armed Forces and National Service personnel. In 1938, the charity opened their flagship training, convalescent and holiday centre in Ovingdean, Brighton, and took delivery of its first coach in 1952. Plaxton Paramount 3200-bodied YMP A523 MJK arrived in 1984 and served St Dunstan's for nearly fifteen years. (AS)

By the time this picture was taken, both Leicester and Burnley & Pendle had dropped out of the City Flyer operation, and the core service had been cut to run between Maidstone and Halifax. Seen on Vauxhall Bridge Road in London, Wright Contour-bodied YNT was new as A210 OKN but soon acquired the registration HKR 11, originally fitted to one of Maidstone's Sunbeam trolleybuses. (AS)

Duple also introduced two new models in 1983 but, unlike Plaxton's Paramount, the Duple's were completely different from each other. The highline Caribbean was aimed at the executive market, and whilst the low-height (and dramatically styled) Laser was available as an exec, it was aimed more at general coach use. Bostock's of Congleton weren't afraid to be amongst the first to order newly introduced bodies or chassis. They ordered one of the first Lasers in 1983 in the shape of YNT A548 RCA, seen arriving at Wembley in 1984. (AS)

The majority of the old-established South Yorkshire independent bus operators ended up being taken over by South Yorkshire PTE or its successor South Yorkshire Transport, with Harold Wilson (Premier) of Stainforth in 1988 being one of the last. The penultimate vehicle delivered to Premier was Plaxton Paramount 3200-bodied YNT A627 YWF, which retained Premier's livery after the takeover, and is seen at SYT's Dunscroft depot. (RS)

In 1991 I moved to Norfolk and took up a management position with Sanders of Holt, so beginning my association with Bedfords, Sanders having nearly sixty in the fleet including examples of every 'Y' type available. New to King's of Dunblane, Plaxton Paramount 3200-bodied YMP B258 AMG was ideal for those private hires which didn't warrant a full-sized coach but required more luxury than a minibus. (HB)

With curves in the right places and dents in the wrong ones, I'm sure a good lick of polish would make Sylvie very happy… This 10-metre Wright Contour-bodied YMP was new to the Soviet Embassy in 1984 as 248-D-276, fitted with thirty-four seats and toilet. By the time it was caught on camera on Eastbourne's Pier Head in 1993 it had passed to Priory of Essex and acquired registration B569 AHX. (AS)

Chambers' YNT B792 MGV, new in 1984, carries the restyled Duple Laser 2 body, introduced at the end of 1984. The main differences being a switch to bonded glazing and a revised front with single headlamps and plastic grille. As Bedford said 'you see them everywhere', as all three vehicles in this view are Bedfords, including St Martin's Scouts Duple Viscount-bodied VAM5 NFM 682E, new as Crosville CVT682 in 1967. (RS).

At one time, National Express contracts were handled solely by NBC subsidiaries, independents being restricted to providing duplicate vehicles at busy times. However, towards the end of the 1980s, independents started to appear on the network as contracted operators. One of the first (and who went on to be one of the largest independent contractors) was Bebb Travel of Llantwit Fardre, whose first coach, painted in full National Express livery, was Duple Laser-bodied YNT B47 DNY, seen in Aylesbury on the Cardiff–Ipswich service. (AS)

Following deregulation of express coach services in 1980, numerous operators introduced express coach services, usually towards London, and Whittle of Highley was no exception, introducing services from the West Midlands under the 'Goldhawk' banner. They were quick to order the Wright Contour, its futuristic styling fitting in well with the image of sleek and efficient coach services, and took six YNTs, most fitted with toilets and catering facilities. 14 (RPP 514) is seen arriving at Victoria coach station in 1984. (AS)

If the Plaxton Derwent bore a resemblance to the Paramount range, then its predecessor, the Bustler, was almost a Supreme with a different front end! Introduced in 1980, all the Bustlers were delivered to independent operators, and whilst it didn't sell in huge numbers, it announced Plaxton's re-entry into the bus market after a gap of five years. Seen in Horsham, YNT B327 KPD was part of Tillingbourne's 1984 intake and was the last full-sized Bustler to be built. (AS)

All Plaxton Paramount-bodied YNTs were of the low-height 3200 model in coach or express variants, and one of the latter is seen here. B124 PEL was new to Tillingbourne in 1984, passing into FirstGroup ownership with Rider York. An internal transfer saw it join South Wales-based Brewer's and, after its revenue-earning days were over, it transferred to Skillplace Training to work as the company's driver training unit. Its manual gearbox made it an ideal vehicle to get that all-important 'all types' licence back when most vehicles tended to be fitted with semi or fully automatic gearboxes. (RS)

France's Motors of Market Weighton was formed in 1927, initially using the name Ideal Motor Services for the coaches and R&J France for the haulage fleet. The two businesses were amalgamated in 1971 and operations continued until the France brothers retired in 2011, selling the business to York Pullman. Seen in the coach park at Scarborough are Plaxton Paramount 3200 YNT B509 YAT and Duple Dominant-bodied YMT RDC 688R. (RS)

One South Yorkshire independent to escape the clutches of SYPTE was Wigmore's of Dinnington, who provided an extremely reliable service to the good people of South Yorkshire. In 1987, the company was sold to new owners and became the basis of what was to become that bastion of second-hand Bristol REs, Northern Bus of North Anston. The last new bus to be bought by Wigmore's was Duple Dominant bus-bodied YNT C472 LKU. New in 1986 in this picture, it had just passed into Northern Bus ownership. (RS)

If there was a prize for the best-presented Bedford coach in Malta, then it must surely go to Cancu Supreme Travel's Plaxton Paramount-bodied YNT BCY 913. New to Willetts of Pillowell in 1987 as D439 GAD, it arrived in Malta in 1993 from Bibby's of Ingleton, whose livery it still carries, even retaining the name *Dales Warrior*. It is seen outside the operator's premises in Zejtun with a Leyland Titan of the open-top fleet for company. I'm guessing the grille forward of the nearside rear wheel probably provides the intake for the air conditioning, which is necessary almost all year round on Malta. (MH)

Bostocks of Congleton's fleet was built on Bedfords, and they purchased them new until the end of production. Plaxton Paramount 3200-bodied YMP E281 XCA was one of the last Bedfords delivered and is seen being put through its paces at the 1988 Brighton Coach Rally. (AS)

Photographed in Dinnington bus station, on tendered bus service 144 to Woodsetts, is Gordon's of Rotherham's D813 SHE, an 8-metre YMP(S) with Plaxton Paramount 3200 body. New to Gordon's in 1987, it passed to ProTours on the Isle of Man in 1998 and was re-registered MAN 111P. (RS)

The Venturer

It is unfortunate that the chassis that could finally have given Bedford back its rightful place in the PSV market arrived just too late to save the marque. Introduced in 1984, the YNV was the first factory-built 12-metre chassis; the first to be fitted with full air suspension (which also allowed for the fitment of a ferry lift), and the first to have a name – Venturer. Still powered by the 8.2-litre 205d engine, as fitted to the YNT and mated to a ZF six-speed gearbox with air-assisted clutch, the Venturer really was a pleasant vehicle to drive. Performance was well up to the standard of the day, and 70 mph motorway cruising seemed effortless, with noise levels well below those of previous chassis. The low unladen weight and extra length meant that operators could now specify coaches built to full executive specification, complete with toilets and drinks servery, whilst utilising a chassis which cost considerably less than its counterparts. There was speculation that the Venturer was also to be made available with the 250 bhp 10-litre Cummins LT10 engine, as this had been made available in the TM range of trucks. However, this failed to materialise and may be one reason why the chassis didn't do as well as Bedford hoped. In the four years the Venturer was offered for sale, just under 250 chassis were sold, the vast majority built in one large batch which took a number of years to sell; in fact one of the first chassis to be built was one of the last to be registered in 1988.

The only Venturer to be fitted with a high-floor 3500 Plaxton Paramount was former demonstrator A247 PGS. The light weight of the chassis caused problems with the tilt-test, and the coach was retro-fitted with a Telma retarder to provide the additional weight required to pass the test. After demonstration duties it spent nearly ten years with Karvien of Walsall before being exported to Ireland. (AS)

The Margo family were heavily involved in the South East London bus and coach scene, with various members of the family running different companies in Penge, Streatham, and as seen here, Bexleyheath. Benson and Gerald Margo ran Bexleyheath Transport until their retirement in 1988 when the company was sold to Moseley's of Loughborough. Over the years they purchased over 130 new Bedfords, usually with seven or eight new coaches entering the fleet every year. Two Venturers from the deliveries made in the two years prior to the sale are Duple Laser-bodied B225 OJU from 1985 and Duple 320-bodied C345 VNR from 1986, both attending the respective year's Brighton Coach Rally. The standard-height Duple 320 and high-floor counterpart the 340 were Duple's replacement for the Laser and Caribbean and were introduced in 1986. (AS)

Whilst the 003 was the last body Willowbrook built in any significant number, they did have one final fling in the mid-1980s with the Crusader. Less than twenty were built, most of which were fitted onto Leyland Leopards that had previously been fitted with 003s! The first one built was Venturer C386 VBC, which was used by Willowbrook as a demonstrator before passing to Silver Service of Darley Dale and is seen here in Leeds on a National Express duplicate, complete with pipe-smoking driver, whilst arriving at Wembley stadium is C32 VJU, delivered new to Cresswell of Moira. (RS/AS)

At the end of 1984, Duple introduced the Laser 2 and Caribbean II (note the different number identifiers for the two models). The main differences were a switch to bonded glazing and a revised front with twin headlamps, and plastic grille instead of the quad headlights and metal grille on the original. One of the last Venturers to be fitted with a Laser 2 was C693 PRA delivered to Felix of Stanley in 1986. (AS)

Probably the only Venturer, nay probably the only Bedford to receive NBC 'venetian blind' livery was Plaxton Paramount 3200-bodied C112 AFX, the newest vehicle in the fleet of New Enterprise of Tunbridge Wells when the company was acquired by Maidstone & District in 1988. New to Excelsior of Bournemouth, it had been purchased by New Enterprise just two days before the takeover took place. (AS)

Whilst Sanders' fleet was predominantly YMTs, ideal vehicles for running around the flatlands of East Anglia on their network of stage carriage services, there was also a large private hire and tour fleet formed of YNTs and Venturers. Another of the ex-Excelsior AFX batch of Plaxton Paramount 3200-bodied Venturers was C115 AFX, identifiable as ex-Excelsior by the absence of the small 'feature window' where the waistrail steps down. (HB)

Seen in the coach park on Mines Road, Laxey, opposite the lovely named Ham & Egg Terrace, are two Plaxton Paramount 3200-bodied Venturers from the Tours (Isle of Man) fleet operating on behalf of Shearings. Both were new to Perret of Shipton Oliffe, F111 MAN nearest the camera as C155 UDD whilst HMN 111 was originally C156 UDD. In the valley behind the coaches is Lady Isabella, the Laxey Wheel, the world's largest water-driven wheel. Constructed in 1854, it was designed to pump water out of the mine workings; back then Laxey was largely a mining village. (RS)

B465 YUR was the only Venturer to receive a Jonckheere body and was used as a demonstration vehicle by Jonckheere's UK dealers Roeselare (so named because Henri Jonckheere began building bodies in that Belgian town in 1881). It is seen on London's Lambeth Bridge in 1995, shortly after being purchased by Smith's of Portland. (PG)

This is one of just four Venturers fitted with Van Hool Alizee bodies. GDZ 5892 was originally registered C413 DML and was also used as a demonstrator, this time by Arlington. It settled down for its first few years with Bakers of Weston-super-Mare but is seen here in the yard of Richard's Coaches of Guist in Norfolk in 2008. (PG)

As mentioned in the YMT section, Banstead Coaches are strong supporters of the Brighton Coach Rally and after winning the Coach Driver of the Year title in 1979, Dudley Haynes has won it a further four times with son Matthew winning once. Their entry in the 1987 rally was Plaxton Paramount 3200-bodied Venturer D72 HRU, a coach which still attends the rally now, still in Banstead Coaches livery. (AS)

Caetano's replacement for the Alpha arrived in 1983 in the shape of the curvaceous Algarve, of which twenty-eight were fitted to Venturers. The sole Algarve-bodied Venturer in Soul's fleet was C88 NNV, new to Hamilton of Stony Stratford in 1986 and acquired along with the company by Souls in 1988. It is seen negotiating Rutland Square in Bakewell. (RS)

Well, there's no doubting what body is fitted to this one! A coach I remember from when it joined the fleet of Graham's of Bristol is Caetano Algarve-bodied Venturer D128 SHE. It was one of a pair delivered to Globe of Barnsley in 1987, both lasting a mere two years in the South Yorkshire fleet, being disposed of in 1989, sister ship D129 SHE passing to Sanders of Holt during my time at that company. (RS)

Despite the close working relationship between the two companies, only three Wright Contours were fitted onto the Venturer chassis, and this is the last of the three. TFE 1R was originally registered D898 TGG and was new to Prentice of West Calder in 1987. Three years later it had travelled south to join the Eagre fleet and is seen parked opposite the depot in Gainsborough. (RS)

Before Avon was abolished as a county in 1996, it operated its own transport fleet, the majority of which were used for home to school welfare transport. They also operated a handful of full-sized coaches, primarily for taking schoolkids to the council-owned swimming baths in Bristol. The last coaches purchased were a pair of Duple 320-bodied Venturers, E251 and 254PEL, which were two of the last five Venturers to be delivered. (AS)

As well as an extensive tour programme, Applebys used their coaches to operate local services, as seen by the Setright machine fitted to Duple 320-bodied Venturer E433 PFU. New to Enterprise & Silver Dawn of Waddington in 1987, it is seen approaching Lincoln bus station on the former Enterprise service to Waddington via Bracebridge Heath. (RS)

New to Capital of West Drayton in 1987 as E245 FLD was Baldry's of Holme on Spalding Moor's Plaxton Paramount 3200-bodied Venturer VIB 4645, which was still in regular use until 2019. It even managed to retain its full set of Bedford badges. It is seen in Pocklington in 2017. (RS)

A company very dear to me is much-missed Great Yarmouth operator Caroline Seagull, as the owner, Mr Buckle, sold me my first coach for preservation back in 1991. Caetano Algarve-bodied Venturer E348 TPW was new to the company in 1988 and is seen in Fort William undertaking a tour for Norwich-based Stirling Holidays, a company Caroline Seagull worked with until ceasing operations in 2008. (RS)

In its heyday, Caroline Seagull purchased numerous ex-East Kent AEC Reliances, all carrying registrations ending in 'FN', which were retained after the coaches were sold or scrapped. E348 TPW received one of these plates, becoming 6541 FN. It received a third number – FBY 001 – when sold to Cauchi Travel on the Maltese archipelago island of Gozo in 1997. It is seen in 2004 carrying the grey and red livery carried by all buses and coaches based on Gozo. (RS)